Greatest Love

Greatest Love

*Unblock Your Life
in 30 Minutes a Day with the
Power of Unconditional Love*

Dr. and Master
Zhi Gang Sha
with
**Master Maya Mackie
and Master Francisco Quintero**

BENBELLA

BenBella Books, Inc.
Dallas, TX

Copyright © 2017 Heaven's Library Publication Corp.
heavenslibrary@drsha.com

Toronto, ON

BenBella Books, Inc.
10440 N. Central Expressway, Suite 800
Dallas, TX 75231
www.benbellabooks.com
Send feedback to feedback@benbellabooks.com.

"Heaven's Library" and "Heart and Soul Series" are trademarks of Heaven's Library Publication Corp.

Printed in the United States of America
10 9 8 7 6 5 4 3 2 1

Library of Congress Cataloging-in-Publication Data is available upon request.
ISBN 9781946885043 (trade cloth)
e-ISBN 9781946885043 (electronic)

Editing by Leah Wilson   Cover design by Henderson Ong
Copyediting by Stacia Seaman   Full cover by Ivy Koval and
Text composition by PerfecType   Sarah Avinger
Proofreading by Michael Fedison   Printed by Lake Book Manufacturing

Distributed by Perseus Distribution
www.perseusdistribution.com

To place orders through Perseus Distribution:
Tel: (800) 343-4499
Fax: (800) 351-5073
E-mail: orderentry@perseusbooks.com

Special discounts for bulk sales (minimum of 25 copies) are available.
Please contact Aida Herrera at aida@benbellabooks.com

Contents

Introduction

HUMANITY AND OUR beloved Mother Earth are facing huge challenges. Climate change resulting from global warming is contributing to ever more frequent and severe natural disasters. There are economic and political challenges, health challenges, and many other challenges. At this historic critical time, how can we help humanity and Mother Earth?

Most of us are deeply concerned about not only our own future but also the future of humanity and Mother Earth herself. Millions of people are searching for ways to help themselves, their loved ones, humanity, and Mother Earth. Millions of people are joining and contributing to all kinds of movements, to spread love and peace, to protect the environment and endangered species, and to help humanity and Mother Earth in other ways.

The purpose of this book is to share with you sacred wisdom and powerful yet simple practices that can empower you to help your loved ones, humanity, and Mother Earth through this challenging period of time.

There is ancient Chinese wisdom, *Tian Ren He Yi*. "Tian" means *big universe*, which includes countless planets, stars, galaxies, and universes, as well as Heaven. Mother Earth is only one planet. Scientists are discovering more and more planets. "Ren" means *human being*, which is the small universe. "He" means *join as*. "Yi" means *one*. "Tian Ren He Yi" (pronounced *tyen wren huh yee*) means *the big universe and human being join as one*.

You may wonder what the significance is of the big universe and human beings joining as one. Currently, Heaven and human beings are not joined as one. They are not in alignment. We believe this is why we are seeing so many natural disasters, economic and political challenges, war, diseases, and more.

Another ancient wisdom is *Shen Qi Jing He Yi*. "Shen" includes soul, heart, and mind. "Qi" means *energy*. "Jing" means *matter*. "He" means *join as*. "Yi" means *one*. "Shen Qi Jing He Yi" (pronounced *shun chee jing huh yee*) means *soul, heart, mind, energy, and matter join as one*.

A human being is made of shen qi jing. Mother Earth is made of shen qi jing. Heaven is made of shen qi jing. A universe is made of shen qi jing. Every cell in a human being, every quark in everything, is made of shen qi jing. *Everyone and everything is made of shen qi jing.*

Why does a person become sick? Because the person's shen qi jing has not joined as one. Why is Mother Earth experiencing such challenges? Because Mother Earth's shen qi jing has not joined as one.

How can we overcome challenges in our health, emotions, relationships, and more? How can we overcome Mother Earth's cha-otic condition? There is a spiritual solution to every challenge that exists. This Heart and Soul Series of books offers sacred wisdom and practice to transform humanity and Mother Earth in every way.

This first book of the Heart and Soul Series, *Greatest Love*, shares a profound wisdom that has been taught throughout the ages by teachers in many traditions. What is this profound wisdom? That the solution to every challenge is greatest love, which is unconditional love. "Da" (pronounced *dah*) means *biggest* or *greatest*. "Ai" (pronounced *eye*) means *love*. The key one-sentence secret that I share with you and humanity is that *love melts all blockages and transforms all life*.

Another ancient wisdom and practice that I share with humanity is *Da Tao Zhi Jian*. "Da" means *big*. "Tao" means *the Way*. "Zhi" means *extremely*. "Jian" means *simple*. "Da Tao Zhi Jian" (pronounced *dah dow jr jyen*) means *the Big Way is extremely simple*. The simple and powerful wisdom, knowledge, and practical techniques shared in the Heart and Soul Series *are* Da Tao Zhi Jian. Many people may think, "Really? The solution for all kinds of challenges for humanity and Mother Earth is so simple?" From my many years of study and personal experience, I say, wholeheartedly, the answer is *yes*.

If you want to know if a pear is sweet, taste it. If you want to know if the Heart and Soul Series is truly a treasure for life transformation, experience it.

Read the book. Do the practices as described. Trust.

You will learn the highest wisdom and experience the simplest and most powerful techniques. Open your heart and soul to receive it.

> *Give it a try.*
> *Practice it.*
> *Experience it.*
> *Benefit from it.*

I love my heart and soul
I love all humanity
Join hearts and souls together
Love, peace, and harmony
Love, peace, and harmony

What Is Greatest Love (Da Ai)?

"DA" MEANS *GREATEST*. "Ai" means *love*. "Da Ai" means *greatest love*. Human love is limited. Da Ai, greatest love, is unlimited and unconditional. To love unconditionally has been the highest calling from teachers of all traditions throughout history.

Da Ai is the first of ten sacred qualities. I am honored to share the deep wisdom and significance of the Ten Da qualities.

In 2013, while I was meditating, I received Ten Da, which are the nature of the Divine and Tao. These sacred qualities include:

1. *Da Ai*, greatest love
   (pronounced *dah eye*)
2. *Da Kuan Shu*, greatest forgiveness
   (pronounced *dah kwahn shoo*)
3. *Da Ci Bei*, greatest compassion
   (pronounced *dah sz bay*)
4. *Da Guang Ming*, greatest light
   (pronounced *dah gwahng ming*)
5. *Da Qian Bei*, greatest humility
   (pronounced *dah chyen bay*)
6. *Da He Xie*, greatest harmony
   (pronounced *dah huh shyeh*)
7. *Da Chang Sheng*, greatest flourishing
   (pronounced *dah chahng shung*)
8. *Da Gan En*, greatest gratitude
   (pronounced *dah gahn un*)
9. *Da Fu Wu*, greatest service
   (pronounced *dah foo woo*)

10. *Da Yuan Man,* greatest enlightenment
    (pronounced *dah ywen mahn*)

Through my spiritual communication channels, I have received four sacred phrases to further explain each of the Ten Da qualities. I will share them in each of the ten books of the Heart and Soul Series, which correspond to the Ten Da.

Heaven explained to me that the Ten Da are the nature of Tao Source, the Creator. They are also the nature of all kinds of saints, buddhas, bodhisattvas, archangels, and more in Heaven. The Ten Da are the highest wisdom and highest practice. They carry the purest shen qi jing of Heaven and Source.

Generally speaking, human beings do not embody these Ten Da qualities in every moment, but everyone has these natures within them. We do not express these qualities freely because our shen qi jing has become polluted.

If a fish lives in polluted water, the fish could become sick and die. This is a very simple fact. To save the fish, we must purify the water. The same is true for human beings. Human beings are sick because they live in polluted environments. It is necessary and important to address all of the pollutions in our world—air pollution, water pollution, food pollution, and more—but the most vital pollution to address is shen qi jing (soul, heart, mind, energy, and matter) pollution, because this pollution accounts for much of the sickness we see today. To help people be happy and healthy, purify their shen qi jing. The Ten Da, which carry the purest shen qi jing, can purify our shen qi jing beyond comprehension.

"Shen" includes soul, heart, and mind. All of these can become polluted or blocked.

Soul pollution and soul blockages include all kinds of negative karma. There are two types of karma: good karma and bad karma.

In every moment, we create bad karma if our words, thoughts, and actions cause harm to another being. This includes gossiping or speaking negatively about others, having unkind thoughts about others, and doing harmful or hurtful things such as lying, cheating, stealing, killing, and taking advantage of others. We have made these types of mistakes and harmed others through our words, thoughts, and actions in all lifetimes, whether intentionally or unintentionally. Because of these mistakes, we have accumulated negative karma, or shen blockages.

Karma is cause and effect, action and reaction. The pain and suffering that we have caused others returns to us in the form of lessons. This is our spiritual debt. On the other hand, we have also created good karma. The good that we have done, including our actions that have helped and served others, our positive thoughts about others, and the uplifting, loving, and encouraging words we have spoken, come back to us as blessings that can enrich every aspect of our lives, bringing us health, happiness, positive energy, intelligence, loving relationships, abundant finances, and more.

Many people believe "what goes around comes around." This is the universal law of karma that applies to everyone and everything. Karma is the root cause of success and failure in every aspect of life. Bad karma or shen (soul) blockages can deeply affect your health, relationships, finances, and more. Good karma will bless your life.

Heart pollution and blockages include greed, jealousy, anger, lack of wisdom in activities, behaviors, speech, and thought, selfishness, and other impurities of the heart.

Mind pollution and blockages include negative mind-sets, negative attitudes, negative beliefs, ego, attachments, and more.

Because human beings have shen qi jing blockages, which are pollution, we are sick and out of balance. To overcome this, we must purify our shen qi jing.

The Ten Da are sacred tools from Heaven and Source to purify one's shen qi jing and to purify the shen qi jing of a family, business, city, country, Mother Earth, and countless planets, stars, galaxies, and universes. A person who applies the Ten Da could receive remarkable purification and transformation in every aspect of life. If an organization applies the Ten Da, the organization could achieve remarkable transformation. If the people in a city were to apply the Ten Da, the city could transform beyond comprehension. If millions of people in Mother Earth would apply the Ten Da, then humanity and Mother Earth could be blessed beyond words.

In one sentence:

Ten Da are sacred wisdom and practical tools that can transform every aspect of life.

Da Ai, greatest love, is the first of the Ten Da. The four sacred phrases of Da Ai are:

一施大愛
Yi Shi Da Ai

無條件愛
Wu Tiao Jian Ai

融化災難
Rong Hua Zai Nan

心清神明
Xin Qing Shen Ming

Yi Shi Da Ai. "Yi" means *first*. "Shi" means *give*. "Da" means *greatest*. "Ai" means *love*. "Yi Shi Da Ai" (pronounced *ee shr dah eye*) means *first give greatest love*.

Wu Tiao Jian Ai. "Wu" means *no*. "Tiao Jian" means *condition*. "Ai" means *love*. "Wu Tiao

Jian Ai" (pronounced *woo tee-yow jyen eye*) means *unconditional love*. The sun, moon, stars, Mother Earth, and Heaven are giving unconditional love in every moment. Tao is the Creator. Tao creates Heaven, Mother Earth, human beings, and countless planets, stars, galaxies, and universes. In every moment, Tao is giving unconditional love. Unconditional love *is* Tao love and Heaven's love. Give unconditional love and you could receive unlimited blessings for health, relationships, financial abundance, business success, and more.

Rong Hua Zai Nan. "Rong Hua" means *melts*. "Zai Nan" means *challenges and disasters*. "Rong Hua Zai Nan" (pronounced *róng hwah dzye nahn*) means *melts all challenges and disasters*. This tells us the benefit of offering unconditional love to others.

Xin Qing Shen Ming. "Xin" means *heart*. "Qing" means *clear* or *transparent*. "Shen"

includes *soul, heart,* and *mind.* "Ming" means
enlightenment. "Xin Qing Shen Ming" (pronounced *sheen ching shun ming*) means *clears
your heart and enlightens soul, heart, and mind.*

The Buddha, Shi Jia Mo Ni Fo (pronounced
shr jyah maw nee fwaw, the Chinese name of
Siddhartha Gautama, the historical Buddha),
taught eighty-four thousand methods to
purify and transform one's life. One of the
most powerful techniques that Shi Jia Mo Ni
Fo taught is *Nian Fo Cheng Fo.* "Nian" means
chant. "Fo" means *Buddha.* "Cheng" means
become. "Nian Fo Cheng Fo" (pronounced
nyen fwaw chung fwaw) means *chant a buddha
to become a buddha.*

A buddha is an enlightened spiritual master and teacher: a saint. A buddha's or saint's
shen qi jing is the purest shen qi jing. To
chant the name of a buddha or saint is to connect with that being's shen qi jing. Their purest shen qi jing can purify your shen qi jing

for transformation of all of your life, including health, relationships, finances, and more.

What you chant is what you become. Da Ai, greatest love, carries the highest and purest shen qi jing of Heaven and Source. As you chant *Da Ai*, your shen qi jing aligns more and more with the shen qi jing of Da Ai. In this book I am sharing that to chant *Da Ai* could transform every aspect of your life. Da Ai's highest and purest shen qi jing could purify and transform your health, relationships, finances, and intelligence beyond any words, comprehension, and imagination.

I have created a CD titled *Da Ai* that can greatly support your chanting practice. You may listen to an excerpt at www.drsha.com/greatestlove. To chant *Da Ai* nonstop is to embody Da Ai. It is to *become* Da Ai.

To uplift and purify our shen qi jing to a purer shen qi jing, we must be aware of our speech, thoughts, and behaviors. Ancient wisdom teaches that a human being's daily life can be described as Shen Kou Yi. Here, "Shen" means *activities* and *behaviors*. "Kou" means *speech*. "Yi" means *thinking*. "Shen Kou Yi" (pronounced *shun koe ee*) means *activities, behaviors, speech, and thoughts*. Shen Kou Yi is divided into positive and negative. It is important for each person to have as much positive Shen Kou Yi as possible. It is important at all times to transform negative Shen Kou Yi to positive Shen Kou Yi.

Every word we speak carries a message. Every word carries shen qi jing. To chant *Da Ai* nonstop is to align with the shen qi jing of Da Ai, greatest love. It is to transform our negative Shen Kou Yi to positive Shen Kou Yi.

In this book, you will learn and practice simple ancient techniques (including chanting powerful mantras such as *Da Ai*) and revolutionary new techniques using Tao Source Calligraphies to empower you to enhance and transform all life. I will lead you to uplift and purify your shen qi jing. To purify your shen qi jing further and further is to transform every aspect of life.

Remember the ancient teaching I shared earlier:

**If you want to know if a
pear is sweet, taste it.**

If you want to know the power of greatest love (Da Ai), experience it.

2

The Power and Significance of Greatest Love (Da Ai)

D A AI, GREATEST love, carries the purest shen qi jing of Heaven, Mother Earth, and human beings. It also carries the purest shen qi jing of Tao Source. Da Ai's purest shen qi jing could enhance your life by:

- boosting energy, stamina, vitality, and immunity

- bringing health and happiness to
  the spiritual, mental, emotional, and
  physical bodies
- rejuvenating the soul, heart, mind, and
  body
- harmonizing relationships
- blessing finances
- increasing intelligence
- opening spiritual channels
- enlightening the soul, heart, mind, and
  body

When you chant *Da Ai*, the purest shen qi jing of Da Ai will purify and transform the shen qi jing of your systems, organs, and cells. It will also purify your DNA and RNA. To chant *Da Ai* nonstop is to bless relationships, finances, intelligence, and every aspect of life.

How does it do this? Da Ai carries a very high frequency and vibration that creates a positive field to transform negative fields to positive fields. It can take time. Transformation is not instant. Some blockages could be transformed faster than others. Some take time. This is a very important reminder that you must be patient and practice persistently and dedicatedly to experience the greatest benefits.

Many people expect instant results or change. In some cases, you *could* experience instant results. But in other cases, more time—even significant time—could be required. The reason is that, for some, the shen qi jing blockages in health, relationships, finances, business, success, and more are very heavy. Therefore, to chant persistently is vital. The more you create the positive field of the purest shen qi jing, the better the results you could achieve.

There is ancient sacred wisdom for spiritual healing and transformation:

Zhou Bu Li Kou

"Zhou" means *mantra*. A mantra is a heal-ing sound or message that is chanted repeat-edly. "Bu" means *not*. "Li" means *leave*. "Kou" means *mouth*. "Zhou Bu Li Kou" (pronounced *joe boo lee koe*) means *the mantra does not leave your mouth*. Chant nonstop. You can chant out loud or silently. Chanting out loud is yang chanting. It vibrates the bigger cells and spaces in the body. Chanting silently is yin chanting. It vibrates the smaller cells and spaces. For many, when you practice silent chanting, it can become a habit. When chant-ing a mantra nonstop becomes a habit, the benefits are enormous. Words are not enough to express the benefits of chanting a mantra nonstop.

You may not be familiar with chanting, and that is perfectly fine. Many traditions around the world repeat a prayer or a special sound or phrase to bring peace, to offer blessings, to express devotion, and more. You can think of chanting as repeating a positive phrase or high-frequency message to bring its blessing.

To chant a mantra is to create a positive field. For example, millions of Buddhists throughout history have chanted *Na Mo A Mi Tuo Fo* (pronounced *nah maw ah mee twaw faw*). "Na Mo" are words of honor to a special esteemed being. They mean *I deeply honor and appreciate you*. "A Mi Tuo Fo" is the name of an ancient buddha.

To chant *Na Mo A Mi Tuo Fo* is to make:

> *A Mi Tuo Fo's heart your heart*
> *A Mi Tuo Fo's soul your soul*
> *A Mi Tuo Fo's mission your mission*
> *A Mi Tuo Fo's service your service*

Chanting *A Mi Tuo Fo* connects you with A Mi Tuo Fo's shen qi jing. He is an enlightened being. His purest shen qi jing—like that of Jesus, Mother Mary, Guan Yin (revered by Buddhists and many others as the

Bodhisattva of Compassion), saints, angels, archangels, gurus, and more—can purify your shen qi jing to enhance health, relationships, finances, intelligence, and more.

Applying this ancient wisdom, chant *Da Ai* to transform your shen qi jing to a purer shen qi jing. The sacred practice is to chant *Da Ai* silently nonstop. The more you silently chant *Da Ai*, the more purification and transformation could happen in every aspect of your life.

3

What Is Tao Source Calligraphy?

CALLIGRAPHY IS ONE of the most revered arts in Chinese culture. For many, it is much more than art. It is spiritual practice.

I learned Yi Bi Zi, a very special and rare form of calligraphy, from Professor Li Qiu Yun, who is more than one hundred years old. She learned Yi Bi Zi from Tai Shi (*supreme teacher*), the teacher of the last emperor of China and the royal family.

"Yi" means *one*. "Bi" means *stroke*. "Zi" means *word*. "Yi Bi Zi" (pronounced *ee bee dz*) means *one stroke accomplishes one word*. Yi Bi Zi is Oneness writing. Traditionally, Chinese words are written using one or more of sixteen different types of strokes, with some Chinese words using twenty or more individual strokes. With Yi Bi Zi, Chinese words and entire phrases are written in one continuous brush stroke.

Yi Bi Zi is the foundation of Tao Source Calligraphy, which is created to bless any aspect of life. Before writing a Tao Source Calligraphy, I connect with spiritual fathers and mothers (saints, buddhas, and more) in Heaven and Source and ask them to bless the writing. After writing Yi Bi Zi, I connect with Heaven, Mother Earth, and countless planets, stars, galaxies, and universes, as well as with Tao Source—the Creator—to bless the calligraphy by transmitting their shen qi jing into the calligraphy. Thus, Tao Source Calligraphy combines the artistic beauty of Yi Bi Zi (fully cursive script, Oneness writing) with Tao light transmissions. Every Tao Calligraphy emits frequencies and vibrations that create a field of light. This positive light field can nourish all aspects of life. Yi Bi Zi—Oneness writing—plus blessings from Heaven and Source become Tao Source Calligraphy. This is how Tao Source Calligraphy is created.

I have taught hundreds of students around the world to write Tao Calligraphy. The life transformation results of applying Tao Calligraphy have been phenomenal. Below are two heart-touching and moving stories.

> *Aloha,*
>
> *A few months ago I started to learn to write Da Ai, greatest love. I had been practicing inconsistently, but then practiced writing for one to two hours a day for three days straight. Something very profound then happened to me that was*

connected to painful heartbreak from years ago.

When I was a young married woman, my first child developed a very severe reaction to some medicine. The result was severe brain damage. I spent my young adult life doing whatever I could, with barely any resources, to care for him. He taught me a great deal about life and determination even though he could not speak, walk, or feed himself, and depended upon his father and me for everything. Regardless of his challenges, he was the light of my life. At the age of nine-and-a-half, he died of breathing complications. I was there with him in the hospital. My heart hurt so much. However, I kept it in and tried to be brave for everyone: my daughters, his classmates and teachers, my friends, everyone.

For many years I threw myself into volunteer work and higher-education pursuits. I was determined to give his life meaning and desperately wanted my family to survive this loss. After a divorce and watching my daughters struggle without a brother and father, my heart ached more and more. I pushed it all inward, and many times cried in silence late at night behind closed doors, never revealing any weakness to my parents and my girls. I felt it was my job to maintain control and strength, or at least maintain the illusion of this. I developed a tough exterior but was still soft inside with a diminishing self-worth.

Many years have passed since then. I worked in many areas of education and have been a strong advocate for quality cultural education for the young as well as the elderly who want to pursue higher education. I've worked for the local university running a successful nationwide scholarship program, provided leadership programming, service learning, and the pursuit of additional resources for Hawaii's schools and native language. I've worked at the federal, state, and county levels to serve the people of Hawaii. My passion to see people empowered to fulfill their dreams and serve their communities has given me great joy. However, there has been a pain in my heart that was deep and never allowed me to be truly happy. As time went on, my time was more for others than my family. Material things became the stand-in for my lack of time for my children.

After a week of learning, tracing, and writing Da Ai, one day I felt as if a switch had been turned on. A light shone so bright that it literally blasted the sadness from my heart. I started to cry as I reflected on my life. I began to remember what had happened to me and what brought me to this sad condition. It was like floodgates opened and I was given permission to be happy once again. I felt a sense of pure joy. As a result, the ache is not there. I feel so much happiness and love for my spouse, my children, my family. It feels like this black hole that had occupied my heart is light. It is truly a miracle to be able to feel this way.

I want to thank Master Sha for bringing Tao Calligraphy to humanity. I've missed so much for all of these years by not loving my husband, children, and family as I should. I have lots of time to make up for, and now I know how to help others who have had this kind of sadness in their life. Tao Calligraphy is a genuine gift from Heaven for all of us, regardless of where you come from or your income level or cultural heritage. I'm deeply grateful for this treasure that is here to serve all humanity.

Try it! You have nothing to lose and everything to gain!

From the bottom of my heart, Da Gan En (greatest gratitude).

Aloha, aloha, aloha,

Malia D.
Maui, Hawaii

I would like to share one of many powerful experiences I have had using the Da Ai Tao Calligraphy. A woman at my workplace collapsed at work one day and was rushed to the hospital with excruciating pain in her leg. She took two weeks off work before returning. About six weeks later she was covering a

day shift and I noticed that she was still limping and looked very stressed.

I asked her how she was, and she told me that she was in extreme and constant pain and that she had fallen at work three more times but had not told anyone because she was worried she would lose her job, being of retirement age. She said that she had been going for physical therapy treatments but it wasn't helping much and she couldn't afford to keep going twice a week. She shared that the issue was related to a large cyst deep inside her leg behind her knee, and that she had been having scans and appointments with doctors about possible surgery.

I told her that I might be able to help her, if not with the pain, at least for the emotional stress she was experiencing. On our break we went to a private room, and I offered her a calligraphy blessing by tracing the Da Ai *Tao Calligraphy in Master Sha's book* Soul Over Matter.[1] *We spent about twenty minutes together. We did forgiveness practice, chanted* Da Ai, *and traced the* Da Ai *calligraphy. Within this time, her pain decreased in intensity from an 8 (on a scale of 1 to 10, with 10 being the worst) to a 3. She said it was the first time she had been able to sit without excruciating pain.*

The next day she came to work looking so much lighter and happier. I noticed over the following weeks that she was walking faster and not hobbling like before. When I saw her three weeks after the calligraphy tracing, she raised her arms in the air and said, "Leonie, I have no pain. I have zero pain!" I asked,

---

[1] Dr. and Master Zhi Gang Sha and Adam Markel: *Soul Over Matter: Ancient and Modern Wisdom and Practical Techniques to Create Unlimited Financial Abundance.* Dallas/Toronto: BenBella Books/Heaven's Library, 2016.

"What has happened?" and she said, "I don't know," as she gave me a big smile and said thank you.

I am so grateful to Master Sha and to the Da Ai Tao Calligraphy. The power of Tao Calligraphy and the power of Da Ai is truly beyond words. We are so incredibly blessed to call upon this power.

Thank you with all my heart and soul.

Leonie
Australia

For this book, I have written a new Tao Source Calligraphy *Da Ai* for you to practice with. See figure 1 (following page 52). Apply this blessing to nourish, unblock, and bring success to every aspect of your life, including to attain health and happiness, give you inner peace, harmonize your relationships, boost your finances, and increase your intelligence. You could significantly transform your life in as little as thirty minutes a day.

How Does Tao Source Calligraphy Work?

I shared earlier that Tao Source Calligraphy carries the shen qi jing of Tao Source. These are the purest and highest frequencies and vibrations of shen qi jing. By tracing or writing this calligraphy, you could receive remarkable results for health, relationships, finances, and every aspect of life because these frequencies can transform our shen qi jing beyond comprehension.

Many teachers and healers talk about frequency and vibration, including how to raise our own frequency and that of the planet in order to become happier and healthier, increase energy, experience abundance, uplift consciousness, and much more. "Everything is frequency. Match the frequency of the reality you want and you cannot help but create that reality. It can be no other way. This is not philosophy. This is physics." This sentiment, often attributed to Albert Einstein, may be apocryphal, but the wisdom is true. To transform some aspect of life, we have to transform our frequency and vibration to a higher and purer frequency and vibration. We have to match (become) that frequency and vibration. As we chant, trace, or write *Da Ai*, our shen qi jing aligns more and more with its purest and highest shen qi jing. This is how Tao Calligraphy works.

In the next chapter, I will lead you to apply the Tao Source Calligraphy *Da Ai*.

4

Apply Tao Source Calligraphy to Enrich and Bless Your Life

TAO SOURCE CALLIGRAPHY is Oneness writing. As I shared in chapter 3, it connects every word in one brush stroke. It also connects with Heaven and countless planets, stars, galaxies, and universes, as well as Tao Source, to pull their purest shen qi jing into the calligraphy. It literally forms a Tao Source positive field of shen qi jing. Therefore, Tao

Source Calligraphy carries power beyond comprehension.

To receive the greatest benefits from Tao Source Calligraphy, apply the Five Power Techniques.

Five Power Techniques

The Five Power Techniques are:

1. **Body Power.** Body Power is to use special hand and body positions for healing, rejuvenation, and transformation.

Hold the fingers of one hand together as in figure 2.

Place the other hand on any area of the body that needs transformation (for example, your heart, kidneys, liver, knee).

2. **Soul Power.** Soul Power is to *say hello*. Everyone and everything has a soul, including your organs, your systems, your cells, other parts of your body, a relationship, your

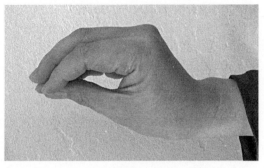

Figure 2. Five Fingers Tracing Power
Hand Position

finances, a mountain, a river, an ocean, and
more.

There are two aspects of saying hello: *say
hello* to inner souls and *say hello* to outer souls.
Here is how to do it.

Say hello to inner souls:

> *Dear shen qi jing of* _____
>   (name the system, organ, part
>   of the body, emotion, etc., that

needs transformation. Or mention a relationship, your finances, or another aspect of your life that needs improvement),

I love you.

You have the power to align with the shen qi jing of Da Ai, greatest love.

Do a great job!

Thank you so much.

Say hello to outer souls:

Dear shen qi jing of Heaven, Mother Earth, and countless planets, stars, galaxies, and universes,

I love you.

Please bless _____ (repeat your request).

Thank you.

Dear Divine,

Dear Tao Source,

I love you.
Please bless _____ *(repeat*
   your request).
Thank you.

Dear Tao Calligraphy Da Ai,
I love you.
Please bless _____ *(repeat*
   your request).
I deeply apologize for all of the mistakes
   that my ancestors and I have made in
   all lifetimes.
I sincerely ask for forgiveness.
I know in my heart and soul that to only
   ask for forgiveness is not enough.
I have to put my service into action.
To serve is to make others happier and
   healthier.
I will serve more and more.
I am very grateful for all of the blessings.
Thank you. Thank you. Thank you.

Forgiveness practice has power beyond words. To transform any condition or blockage in your life, it is vital to do forgiveness practice regularly. Sincere forgiveness practice could self-clear shen qi jing blockages beyond comprehension.

There are two aspects of forgiveness practice:

- asking for forgiveness for your and your ancestors' mistakes in all lifetimes
- offering forgiveness to those who have made mistakes against you and your ancestors in all lifetimes

Here is how to do it:

> *Dear all the souls my ancestors and I have hurt, harmed, or taken advantage of in any way in this lifetime and in past lifetimes,*

Please forgive my ancestors and me for
    our mistakes against you.
I am deeply sorry.
I offer my unconditional forgiveness to
    all souls who have hurt me and my
    ancestors in all lifetimes.
Please accept my forgiveness.
I forgive you.
Please forgive me.
Bring love, peace, and harmony.
Thank you. Thank you. Thank you.

3.   **Sound Power.** Sound Power is to repeatedly chant or sing special mantras or vibratory sounds for health, happiness, rejuvenation, inner peace, nourishment, purification, and enrichment.

   Chant or sing repeatedly:

Da Ai, Da Ai (pronounced *dah eye*)
Da Ai, Da Ai

Da Ai, Da Ai
Da Ai, Da Ai . . .

Greatest love
Greatest love
Greatest love
Greatest love . . .

4.   **Mind Power.** Mind Power is creative visualization. Visualize golden light shining on the area of your request, whether it be a part of your body, a relationship, your finances, or any aspect of your life.

5.   **Tao Source Calligraphy Tracing Power.** Tracing Power is to connect with and receive the frequency and vibration of Tao Source shen qi jing. When you do this, you are nourishing and removing blockages in your shen qi jing. Your shen qi jing will be more balanced and harmonized, which could benefit

your health, emotions, intelligence, relation-
ships, finances, and more in a profound way.
See figure 3 to learn the pathway to trace the
Da Ai calligraphy in figure 1.

Figure 3. Oneness path of Tao
Source Calligraphy *Da Ai*

Hold the fingers of one hand together as shown in figure 2 to trace the *Da Ai* calligraphy. See figure 3 above for the tracing pathway. At the same time, chant *Da Ai*. Chant from your heart with great love.

Trace for ten minutes per time, at least three times per day. There is no time limit. You can trace as often as you can for as long as you can. The more you practice, the better the results you could achieve. For chronic and life-threatening conditions, trace two hours or more per day. You can add all of the tracing time together to total two hours per day.

There is one other way to trace the Tao Source Calligraphy *Da Ai*, and that is to trace using the abdomen and hips.

Millions of people worldwide practice the sacred ancient movement and wisdom of tai ji to benefit their health and for stress reduction, longevity, and more.

I created a special movement named *Tao Shu Fa Tai Ji Yang Sheng*. "Tao" is the Source.

"Shu Fa" means *calligraphy*. "Tai Ji" is an ancient internal movement practice, originally developed as a martial art. "Yang Sheng" means *nourishment, rejuvenation, purification, and healing*. "Tao Shu Fa Tai Ji Yang Sheng" (pronounced *dow shoo fa tye jee yahng shung*) means *Tao Calligraphy Tai Ji movement for nourishment, rejuvenation, purification, and healing*. See figure 4.

You can watch a video of Tao Shu Fa Tai Ji Yang Sheng at www.drsha.com/greatestlove.

Figure 4. Tao Shu Fa Tai Ji Yang Sheng

The Five Power Techniques are *Wu Mi He Yi*. "Wu" means *five*. "Mi" means *secret*. "He" means *join as*. "Yi" means *one*. "Wu Mi He Yi" (pronounced *woo mee huh ee*) means *join the secret and sacred Five Power Techniques as one* or *apply all Five Power Techniques together*.

The practice of applying Tao Calligraphy is very simple and can be used to bring nourishment to any part of the body, to your emotions, to a relationship, or to any aspect of your life. I will lead you in a few practices now. Here is the way to do it.

Self-healing for the Back

Millions of people suffer from back pain and other back issues. What is the reason for this? Shen qi jing blockages. Their shen qi jing is not aligned as one.

Body Power. Face the *Da Ai* calligraphy (figure 1). Hold the fingers of one hand together

in the Five Fingers Tracing Power Hand
Position (figure 2, page 37).

Then *say hello*:

Soul Power. *Say hello* to inner souls:

> *Dear shen qi jing of my back,*
> *I love you.*
> *You have the power to enrich, nourish,*
> *   and heal yourself.*
> *Do a great job!*
> *Thank you.*

Say hello to outer souls:

> *Dear Divine and Tao Source,*
> *My name is _____.*
> *I deeply apologize for all of the mistakes*
> *   that my ancestors and I have made in*
> *   all lifetimes.*
> *I ask for forgiveness for my ancestors*
> *   and me.*

*I know in my heart and soul to only ask
   for forgiveness is not enough.*
I have to serve.
I will serve.
*To serve is to make others happier and
   healthier.*
I will serve more and more.
I am very grateful for all the blessings.
Thank you so much.

*Dear all souls whom my ancestors and I
   have hurt, harmed, or taken advantage of in any way in this lifetime and
   in past lifetimes,*
*Please forgive my ancestors and me for
   our mistakes against you.*
I am deeply sorry.
*I offer my unconditional forgiveness to
   all souls who have hurt me and my
   ancestors in all lifetimes.*
Please accept my forgiveness.
I forgive you.

Please forgive me.
Bring love, peace, and harmony.
Thank you. Thank you. Thank you.

Dear shen qi jing of the Tao Calligraphy
    Da Ai,
I love you.
Please bless _____ (state your
    request for your back).
I am very grateful.

Mind Power. Visualize golden light shining in your back.

Tao Source Calligraphy Tracing Power. See figure 1, the Tao Source Calligraphy *Da Ai*. Trace the *Da Ai* calligraphy following the oneness pathway shown in figure 3. You can trace with your hand as in figure 2 or with your body as in figure 4.

Sound Power. Chant or sing repeatedly:

Da Ai, Da Ai
Da Ai, Da Ai
Da Ai, Da Ai
Da Ai, Da Ai . . .

Greatest love
Greatest love
Greatest love
Greatest love . . .

Trace for ten minutes per time, at least three times per day. There is no time limit. You can trace as often as you can for as long as you can. The more you practice, the better the results you could achieve. For severe and chronic back conditions, trace two hours or more per day. You can add all of the tracing time together to total two hours per day.

There are thousands of heart-touching and moving stories from tracing and writing Tao Calligraphy. Here is a story about how one person's chronic back pain improved from tracing Tao Calligraphy:

> *In 2014, I was suffering from a great deal of back pain. I had been to two neurosurgeons, and both recommended back surgery for my condition, which was confirmed by MRIs and CT scans. I had been advised that without surgery, my back situation would only get worse. I honestly did not want to undergo such an extensive surgery.*
>
> *I had been to physical therapy and had taken anti-inflammatory medicines, as well as some pain medication when needed.*

I received a calligraphy for spinal column healing and traced it diligently. I am happy to report that my back pain has improved 90–95 percent and I am almost pain-free!

I am so thankful. It is a true gift, and I want to thank Master Sha for sharing these gifts that God has blessed him with. Thank you, Jesus!

Diane L.
California

Self-healing for Anger

As another example of self-healing with Tao Source Calligraphy, let us focus on transforming blockages related to anger.

Figure 1. Tao Source Calligraphy *Da Ai*

Body Power. Face the *Da Ai* calligraphy (figure 1). Hold the fingers of one hand together in the Five Fingers Tracing Power Hand Position (see figure 2). Place the other hand on the liver. Traditional Chinese medicine teaches that the liver connects with anger in the emotional body.

Soul Power. *Say hello* to your inner souls:

> *Dear shen qi jing of my liver,*
> *I love you.*
> *You have some blockages.*
> *You have the power to clear these blockages.*
> *You have the power to align with the shen qi jing of Da Ai, greatest love.*
> *Do a great job!*
> *Thank you.*

Say hello to outer souls:

Dear shen qi jing of Heaven, Mother Earth, and countless planets, stars, galaxies, and universes,
I love you.
Please bless my liver and transform my anger and irritation.
Thank you.

Dear Divine and Tao Source,
My name is _____.
I deeply apologize for all of the mistakes that my ancestors and I have made in all lifetimes.
I ask for forgiveness for my ancestors and me.
I know in my heart and soul that to only ask for forgiveness is not enough.
I have to serve.
I will serve.
To serve is to make others happier and healthier.
I will serve more.

I am so grateful for your blessings.
Thank you so much.

Dear all souls whom my ancestors and I
 have hurt, harmed, or taken advan-
 tage of in any way in this lifetime and
 in past lifetimes,
Please forgive my ancestors and me for
 our mistakes against you.
I am deeply sorry.
I offer my unconditional forgiveness to
 all souls who have hurt or harmed
 my ancestors and me in all lifetimes.
Please accept my forgiveness.
I forgive you.
Please forgive me.
Bring love, peace, and harmony.
Thank you. Thank you. Thank you.

Dear shen qi jing of Divine, Tao, and the
 Tao Source Calligraphy Da Ai,
I love you.

*You have the power to reduce and
    remove my anger with your nourish-
    ment, frequency, and vibration.
I am very grateful.
Thank you so much.*

Sound Power. Chant or sing repeatedly with love:

*Da Ai, Da Ai
Da Ai, Da Ai
Da Ai, Da Ai
Da Ai, Da Ai . . .*

*Greatest love
Greatest love
Greatest love
Greatest love . . .*

Mind Power. Visualize bright golden light shining in the liver.

Tao Source Calligraphy Tracing Power. Trace the *Da Ai* calligraphy with all five fingers of one hand together (figure 2) following the oneness pathway shown in figure 3. You can trace with your hand or you can trace with your body as in figure 4. At the same time, chant *Da Ai*.

Trace and chant for ten minutes per time, at least three times per day. For severe and chronic anger, trace two hours or more per day. You can add all of the tracing time together to total two hours per day.

Self-healing for Depression and Anxiety

Millions of people on Mother Earth suffer from depression and anxiety. These conditions are related to shen qi jing blockages in the heart.

Body Power. Face the calligraphy (figure 1) and hold the fingers of one hand together as in the Five Fingers Tracing Power Hand

Position (figure 2). Gently cover the heart with the palm of the other hand. Traditional Chinese medicine teaches that the heart connects with depression and anxiety in the emotional body.

Soul Power. *Say hello* to inner souls:

> *Dear shen qi jing of my heart,*
> *I love you.*
> *You have some blockages.*
> *You can clear these blockages by yourself.*
> *Do a great job!*
> *Thank you so much.*

Say hello to outer souls:

> *Dear Divine and Tao Source,*
> *My name is* _____.
> *I deeply apologize for all of the mistakes*
> *that my ancestors and I have made in*
> *all lifetimes.*

*I ask for forgiveness for my ancestors
    and me.*
*I know in my heart and soul that to only
    ask for forgiveness is not enough.*
I have to serve.
I will serve.
*To serve is to make others happier and
    healthier.*
Please bless me.
Thank you so much.

*Dear all souls whom my ancestors and I
    have hurt, harmed, or taken advan-
    tage of in any way in this lifetime and
    in past lifetimes,*
*Please forgive my ancestors and me for
    our mistakes against you.*
I am deeply sorry.
*I offer my unconditional forgiveness to
    all souls who have hurt me and my
    ancestors in all lifetimes.*
Please accept my forgiveness.

I forgive you.
Please forgive me.
Bring love, peace, and harmony.
Thank you. Thank you. Thank you.

Dear shen qi jing of Divine, Tao, and the
    Tao Source Calligraphy Da Ai,
I love you.
You have the power to heal my depres-
    sion and anxiety.
I am very grateful.
Thank you so much.

Sound Power. Chant or sing repeatedly with love:

Da Ai, Da Ai
Da Ai, Da Ai
Da Ai, Da Ai
Da Ai, Da Ai . . .

Greatest love
Greatest love
Greatest love
Greatest love . . .

Mind Power. Visualize bright golden light shining and radiating in the heart.

Tao Source Calligraphy Tracing Power. Face the *Da Ai* calligraphy. Trace the calligraphy with all five fingers of one hand together as in the Five Fingers Tracing Hand Position (see figure 2). You can also trace with your body as in figure 4. Follow the oneness pathway shown in figure 3. At the same time, chant *Da Ai*.

Trace and chant ten minutes per time, at least three times per day. For severe and chronic depression or anxiety, trace two hours or more per day. Add all of the tracing time together to total two hours.

This teenager's chronic anxiety was transformed with Tao Calligraphy:

*Two months ago, I offered Tao
Calligraphy tracing service for the
teenage son of one of my students. She
explained that her son had deep anxiety
and worry in many aspects of his life.
His relationships with his friends were
especially shadowed by these feelings.*

*Just over a month later, the mother
contacted me with this note:*

Since you offered the calligraphy tracing for my son,
he started to change very
favorably. He is much more
social now. It is as if he
suddenly grew up. He has

self-confidence now. Thank
you so very much.

*Thank you, Master Sha! Thank you,
Tao Calligraphy! Thank you, Divine and
Tao Source!*

E. O.

Self-healing for Any Condition

There are so many kinds of challenges in the
physical body, emotional body, mental body,
and spiritual body. In my teaching, love melts
all blockages and transforms all life. Da Ai,
greatest love, can transform all kinds of challenges and blockages.

Body Power. Face the *Da Ai* calligraphy. Hold
the fingers of one hand together in the Five
Fingers Tracing Power Hand Position (figure

2). Place your other hand over the area that needs health, happiness, rejuvenation, inner peace, nourishment, purification, unblocking, and enrichment.

Soul Power. *Say hello* to inner souls:

> *Dear shen qi jing of my* _____
>   (name the area for which you are
>   requesting the blessing),
> *I love you.*
> *You have some blockages.*
> *You can clear these blockages by yourself.*
> *Do a great job!*
> *Thank you.*

Say hello to outer souls:

> *Dear Divine and Tao Source,*
> *My name is* _____.
> *I deeply apologize for all of the mistakes*
>   *that my ancestors and I have made in*
>   *all lifetimes.*

*I ask for forgiveness for my ancestors
and me.*
*I know in my heart and soul to only ask
for forgiveness is not enough.*
I have to serve.
I will serve.
*To serve is to make others happier and
healthier.*
I am so grateful for all the blessings.
Thank you so much.

*Dear all souls whom my ancestors and I
have hurt, harmed, or taken advantage of in any way in this lifetime and
in all past lifetimes,*
*Please forgive my ancestors and me for
our mistakes against you.*
I am deeply sorry.
*I offer my unconditional forgiveness to
all souls who have hurt or harmed
my ancestors and me in all lifetimes.*
Please accept my forgiveness.

I forgive you.
Please forgive me.
Bring love, peace, and harmony.
Thank you. Thank you. Thank you.

Dear shen qi jing of Divine, Tao, and the
  Tao Source Calligraphy Da Ai,
I love you.
Please bless my _____ (name
  the area of the body or
  condition).
Please nourish, enrich, and bless me as
  appropriate.
I am very grateful.
Thank you so much.

Sound Power. Chant or sing with greatest love:

Da Ai, Da Ai
Da Ai, Da Ai

Da Ai, Da Ai
Da Ai, Da Ai . . .

Greatest love
Greatest love
Greatest love
Greatest love . . .

Mind Power. Visualize bright golden light shining in the area of your request.

Tao Source Calligraphy Tracing Power. Trace the *Da Ai* calligraphy (figure 1) with the five fingers of one hand joined together as in the Five Fingers Tracing Power Hand Position in figure 2. Follow the pathway shown in figure 3. At the same time, chant *Da Ai*. You can also trace with the body as in figure 4.

Trace ten minutes per time, at least three times per day. For chronic and serious conditions, trace for two hours or more per day. You can trace throughout the day and add all of the tracing time together to equal two hours or more per day.

Enrich and Harmonize Relationships

Relationships play a major role in our lives. Humanity has all kinds of challenges in relationships, including family relationships, workplace relationships, relationships between friends, relationships between organizations, relationships between countries, relationships between religions, and more.

I emphasize again the four sacred phrases that carry the wisdom of Da Ai:

Yi Shi Da Ai
Wu Tiao Jian Ai
Rong Hua Zai Nan
Xin Qing Shen Ming

First give greatest love
Unconditional love

Melts all disasters and challenges
Clears your heart and enlightens
your soul, heart, and mind

Therefore, chanting and tracing *Da Ai* could offer love, peace, and harmony for all kinds of relationships. Remember the teaching I shared earlier, Da Tao Zhi Jian, *the Big Way is extremely simple.*

You could experience great transformation from this simple and powerful practice. Da Ai can melt blockages and challenges in any aspect of life, including all kinds of relationships and much more. Apply the wisdom.

Trust it.

Practice it.

Experience it.

Benefit from it.

Let us do it.

Body Power. Face the *Da Ai* calligraphy. Hold the fingers of one hand together in the Five

Fingers Tracing Power Hand Position (see figure 2). Put the palm of your other hand over your root chakra, a fist-sized energy center located at the bottom of the torso that connects with relationships (see figure 5). Think of the relationship you would like to bless.

Soul Power. *Say hello* to inner souls:

> *Dear shen qi jing of my root chakra,*
> *Dear soul, heart, mind, and body of*
>   _____ (name the other
>   person, organization, or whomever you wish to have a more harmonized relationship with),
> *I love you.*
> *We have some blockages.*
> *Let us clear these blockages together.*

Say hello to outer souls:

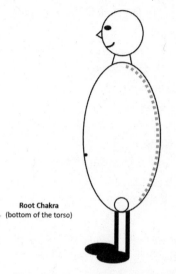

Root Chakra
(bottom of the torso)

Figure 5. First (Root) Chakra

Dear Divine and Tao Source,
My name is _____.
I deeply apologize for all of the mistakes
that my ancestors and I have made in
all lifetimes.

I ask for forgiveness for my ancestors
    and me.
I know in my heart and soul to only ask
    for forgiveness is not enough.
I have to serve.
I will serve.
To serve is to make others happier and
    healthier.
Please bless my relationship with

    _____.

Thank you so much.

Dear shen qi jing of Divine, Tao, and the
    Tao Source Calligraphy Da Ai,
I love you.
You have the power to transform my
    relationship with _____.
I am very grateful for your blessings.
Thank you.

Dear _____ *(name the per-*
    son, organization, or whomever

you wish to harmonize your relationship with),

I love you.

*Please forgive my ancestors and me for
all mistakes we have made against
you in all lifetimes.*

Please forgive _____ *(if there
is something specific you wish to
ask for forgiveness for, you can
name it).*

I am deeply sorry.

*I offer you my unconditional forgiveness
for all your mistakes to my ancestors
and me in this lifetime and in all past
lifetimes.*

I forgive you.

Please forgive me.

Bring love, peace, and harmony.

Thank you. Thank you. Thank you.

Sound Power. Chant or sing from your heart
with greatest love:

Da Ai, Da Ai
Da Ai, Da Ai
Da Ai, Da Ai
Da Ai, Da Ai . . .

Greatest love
Greatest love
Greatest love
Greatest love . . .

Mind Power. Visualize bright golden light shining in the first chakra.

Tao Source Calligraphy Tracing Power. Trace the *Da Ai* calligraphy with all five fingers of one hand together as in the Five Fingers Tracing Power Hand Position (figure 2) following the oneness pathway shown in figure 3. You can also trace with your body as in figure 4. At the same time, chant *Da Ai*.

Trace ten minutes per time, at least three times per day. For severe relationship challenges, you can trace and chant much more.

There are thousands of heart-touching stories from tracing Tao Calligraphy. Here is a story about how a relationship was transformed from tracing Tao Calligraphy:

> In August 2016, I offered Tao Source Calligraphy tracing service to a client for his parents' hearts.
>
> He explained to me that his parents had been on the brink of divorce. They were constantly quarreling and did not want to stay together anymore. They were already in their seventies, but the situation was extremely unbearable for both of them. They felt there was no other option than to separate.

I traced for his parents' hearts (and his) five times remotely within a week, tracing for ten minutes each time.

A month later, this gentleman reported that his parents' relationship had totally transformed. He further explained that "they were like in the days of their honeymoon."

Thank you, Master Sha and Tao Calligraphy!

E.O.

Enrich and Bring Abundance to Finances

Financial challenges are one of the major blockages for humanity. Around the world, many people have no job or struggle to make ends meet. Da Ai, greatest love, can melt all kinds of blockages, including financial blockages.

Here is an amazing story of financial abundance from tracing Tao Calligraphy:

> *Sports 1 Marketing is one of the most notable sports marketing companies in the world. We represent some of the biggest companies in the world, including L'Oréal and Greenbrier Resorts, and we represent athletes, celebrities, and entertainers. We help market the Football Hall of Fame, and we work with entities and major events like the Super Bowl, the Pro Bowl, the NFL Players Association, the Masters, the Kentucky Derby, and the Breeders' Cup. We also work with award shows like the ESPYs, the Emmys, the Oscars, and film festivals like Cannes, Tribeca, and Newport Beach, as well as over 5,700 charitable golf tournaments and galas.*

I received my first Tao Calligraphy from Master Sha. He was in my office explaining the power of Tao Source Calligraphy and literally took out a big piece of paper, spread it on our conference room table, and wrote a calligraphy. When I heard how valuable this calligraphy was, it gained my interest. But I have to tell you, I did not find out how truly valuable this calligraphy was until I actually started to trace it myself.

Master Sha explained to me that if I traced the calligraphy with my five fingers, I could actually benefit much more than if I just kept the calligraphy up in my office. I started tracing once a day.

I felt different. Things started happening. Our business was successful, but it became extremely successful. I mean millions of dollars more, and there was no stopping it. I started to not only trace once a day. I trace ten times a day. First thing in the morning, I trace Master Sha's calligraphy ten times. Without any resistance, almost miraculous things happen for my business. I have always been successful, but there was always hard work, obstacles, shortages—all these resistant energies. After tracing the calligraphy, I feel that everything is going to come to me in the right way at the perfect time. In fact, one of my favorite stories is that we grew from about five employees and about five to ten interns when I met Master Sha. Now we have almost fifty people in my office. And we have experienced exponential growth, to the point that everyone is so busy.

One of my favorite employees approached me while I was tracing the calligraphy one day and said, "Please stop."

I said, "What are you talking about? This is awesome."

He said, "Please, we cannot handle any more business."

Master Sha originally gave me a calligraphy of my choice. Of course, I asked for one for financial success. Because of the great success I have experienced from tracing the calligraphy, I asked if he could write a second one for my family. I now have one of Master Sha's calligraphies in my dining room. Every morning before I leave for work, I trace it at least ten times as well. I also have a calligraphy book, which has many calligraphies and explanations in it.

I have not been sick since the day I met Master Sha. My energy level has been incredible, as well as my family life and my relationships. I know I participate in the transformation as I have been tracing every day, but these calligraphies are two of the most valuable things in my life.

Dave Meltzer
CEO of Sports 1 Marketing

Let us practice together now.

Body Power. Face the *Da Ai* calligraphy. Hold the fingers of one hand together in the Five Fingers Tracing Power Hand Position (see figure 2). Gently cover the heart chakra with the other palm. The heart chakra is a fist-sized energy center located in the center of the chest, behind the sternum (see figure 6). It connects with your finances.

Soul Power. *Say hello* to inner souls:

> *Dear shen qi jing of my heart chakra,*
> *I love you.*
> *You have some challenges.*
> *You have the power to clear these challenges by yourself.*
> *Do a great job!*
> *Thank you.*

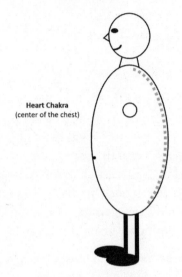

Heart Chakra
(center of the chest)

Figure 6. Heart chakra

Say hello to outer souls:

Dear Divine and Tao Source,
My name is _____.

I deeply apologize for all of the mistakes
*   that my ancestors and I have made in*
*   all lifetimes.*
Please forgive my ancestors and me.
I know in my heart and soul to only ask
*   for forgiveness is not enough.*
I have to serve.
To serve is to make others happier and
*   healthier.*
I am grateful for your blessings.
Thank you so much.

Dear all souls whom my ancestors and I
*   have hurt, harmed, or taken advan-*
*   tage of in any way in this lifetime and*
*   in all lifetimes,*
Please forgive my ancestors and me for
*   our mistakes against you.*
I am deeply sorry.
I offer my unconditional forgiveness to
*   all souls who have hurt or harmed*
*   my ancestors and me in all lifetimes.*

Please accept my forgiveness.
I forgive you.
Please forgive me.
Bring love, peace, and harmony.
Thank you. Thank you. Thank you.

Dear shen qi jing of Divine, Tao, and the
    Tao Source Calligraphy Da Ai,
Dear shen qi jing of countless planets,
    stars, galaxies, and universes,
I love you.
You have the power to transform my
    finances.
Please bless my finances.
I am very grateful.
Thank you.

Sound Power. Chant or sing with love:

Da Ai, Da Ai
Da Ai, Da Ai

Da Ai, Da Ai
Da Ai, Da Ai . . .

Greatest love
Greatest love
Greatest love
Greatest love . . .

Mind Power. Visualize brilliant golden light shining in your heart chakra.

Tao Source Calligraphy Tracing Power. Apply the Five Fingers Tracing Power Hand Position (figure 2) to trace the *Da Ai* calligraphy following the pathway in figure 3. Chant *Da Ai* while you trace. You can also trace with the body.

Trace ten minutes per time, at least three times per day. If your financial situation is extremely challenging, you could trace for two or more hours per day. You can add all of the tracing and chanting time together to equal two hours.

Do the practice with sincerity and with love. Sincerity moves Heaven.

Modify the exercises in this chapter for your particular needs for health, happiness, rejuvenation, inner peace, nourishment, purification, and enrichment.

Remember, Da Ai, greatest love, has power beyond comprehension.

Chant from your heart. Trust. Trace. Chant.

I wish you greatest success!

5

Chant and Trace Tao Calligraphy to Serve Humanity and Mother Earth

IN THE LAST decade, we have experienced more and more natural disasters on Mother Earth, including earthquakes, tsunamis, volcanic eruptions, hurricanes, and more. Global warming has increased rapidly. We have also experienced more and more economic and political challenges. At the same time, some cities and countries have experienced serious air pollution, water pollution, and other kinds of pollution.

How can we help humanity?

Let me emphasize the ancient wisdom I shared in the beginning of this book.

Everyone and everything is made of shen qi jing. As I shared earlier, "shen" includes soul, heart, and mind. "Qi" is *energy*. "Jing" is *matter*. We are used to thinking about energy and matter. In Einstein's theory of relativity, $E = mc^2$, "E" denotes *energy*, "m" denotes *matter*, and "c" is *the speed of light*. Relativity is the relationship between qi and jing. But now is the time for science and humanity to pay attention to shen.

Spiritual teachings use the term *soul* or *spirit*. Science, including quantum physics, uses the term *information* or *message*. In my personal opinion, information or message *is* soul or spirit. They are different names for the same thing. They are one. If people could understand they are the same, science and spirituality could then unite as one.

Dr. and Master Rulin Xiu and I have written a breakthrough book, *Soul Mind Body Science System: Grand Unification Theory and Practice for Healing, Rejuvenation, Longevity, and Immortality*.[2] In it we share with humanity the grand unification scientific equation:

$$S + E + M = 1$$

"S" represents *shen*, which includes soul, heart, and mind. "E" means *energy*. "M" means *matter*. "1" is the Tao Source Oneness Field.

We explain in *Soul Mind Body Science System* that people get sick because their soul, heart, mind, and body are not joined as one. Their S + E + M are not equal to 1. We share many profound secrets within that book.

_____

[2] Dallas/Toronto: BenBella Books/Heaven's Library, 2014.

These secrets explain very well how Divine and Tao Source serve humanity, Mother Earth, and countless planets, stars, galaxies, and universes.

Let me explain further. Everyone and everything is made of shen qi jing, including human beings, animals, oceans, mountains, houses, this book, Mother Earth, and countless planets, stars, galaxies, and universes. I will use a human being as an example to explain this profound secret.

A human being is made of shen qi jing. See figure 7.

There are four sacred phrases that I believe are the absolute truth:

1. **Qi Dao Xue Dao**

"Qi" means *energy*. "Xue" means *blood*. "Dao" means *arrive*. "Qi Dao Xue Dao" (pronounced *chee dow shoo-eh dow*) means *energy arrives, blood follows*. Qi leads blood, which is matter or jing.

Figure 7. Relationship of Shen Qi
Jing in four sacred phrases

This explains the relationship between qi
and jing (energy and matter).

2. **Yi Dao Qi Dao**

"Yi" means *consciousness*. There are many
kinds of consciousness, including superficial

consciousness, deep consciousness, super-consciousness, and subconsciousness.

Millions of people meditate. To meditate is to transform consciousness. In the last decade or more, mind over matter and mindfulness have become more and more popular. To practice mind over matter and mindfulness is to apply the power of the mind and conscious awareness to transform aspects of one's life, including health, relationships, finances, and more. Mind-over-matter techniques include many types of meditation, positive thinking, creative visualization, imagery, and more.

"Yi Dao Qi Dao" (pronounced *ee dow chee dow*) means *consciousness leads qi*. If consciousness arrives, then energy follows.

3. **Xin Dao Yi Dao**

"Xin" means *heart*. In ancient wisdom, the heart houses the soul and mind. There is also an ancient sacred phrase: *Xin Xiang Shi Cheng*.

"Xin" means *heart*. "Xiang" means *think*. "Shi" means *things*. "Cheng" means *accomplish*. "Xin Xiang Shi Cheng" (pronounced *sheen shyahng shr chung*) means *heart thinks, things are done*. This is a very high-level wisdom and spiritual power.

"Xin Dao Yi Dao" (pronounced *sheen dow ee dow*) means *heart arrives, mind (consciousness) follows*. Heart leads consciousness. This profound secret is vital to treating mental disorders. Many people think that mental disorders are connected with the brain or consciousness. In fact, to heal mental disorders, it is vital to remove heart blockages, which is ancient sacred wisdom and practice.

Heart is the boss of the mind. Heart leads the mind.

4. Ling Dao Xin Dao

"Ling" means *soul* or *spirit*. Soul is the top boss of a human being. Many people think that they do what their mind guides them to do. They may not realize that their soul or spirit is the boss of their heart, and thus their mind. Whatever you do, your soul is involved. If your soul agrees with your heart and mind, things will more likely be smooth. If your soul does not agree with your heart and mind, things will more likely be blocked.

"Ling Dao Xin Dao" (pronounced *ling dow sheen dow*) means *soul or spirit* (or *information or message*) *arrives, heart follows*. Soul is the boss of the heart.

These four sacred phrases are four of the highest truths that explain how our shen qi jing is interrelated. It can be simply illustrated as follows:

Soul (message) ➡ Heart ➡ Mind ➡ Energy ➡ Matter

In one sentence:

**Shen is the boss of a human being,
but soul is the ultimate boss.**

I wrote this chapter to call you and humanity to chant *Da Ai* to help humanity and Mother Earth pass through this difficult period of time.

Humanity and Mother Earth need Da Ai. We have created the Love Peace Harmony Movement and Love Peace Harmony World Family. You can learn more about events and opportunities to chant and more to create and manifest love, peace, and harmony for humanity and all souls by joining us at www.lovepeaceharmony.org.

The purpose of life is to serve. I have committed my life to this purpose. To serve is to make others happier and healthier. To chant *Da Ai* is to offer your greatest service to humanity, to countless souls, to the Divine, and to Tao Source.

This is how to do it.

Apply the Five Power Techniques.

Body Power. Face the *Da Ai* calligraphy. Hold the fingers of one hand together in the Five Fingers Tracing Power Hand Position (see figure 2). Put your other palm gently over your heart. You connect with humanity and all souls through your heart.

Soul Power. *Say hello* to inner souls:

> *Dear shen qi jing of my heart,*
> *I love you.*
> *I would like to serve humanity and*
>   *Mother Earth.*
> *Let's do it together.*

Say hello to outer souls:

*Dear shen qi jing of Divine, Tao, and the
    Tao Source Calligraphy* Da Ai,
*Dear shen qi jing of countless planets,
    stars, galaxies, and universes,*
*Dear my family, loved ones, community,
    city, and country,*
Dear humanity and all souls,
I love you all.
*You have the power to transform
    humanity, Mother Earth, and count-
    less planets, stars, galaxies, and
    universes.*
Please join me to chant Da Ai *together.*
Let us do a great job together!
I am deeply grateful.
Thank you.

*Dear all souls whom my ancestors and I
    have hurt, harmed, or taken advan-
    tage of in any way in this lifetime and
    in all past lifetimes,*

*Please forgive my ancestors and me for
    our mistakes against you.
I am deeply sorry for your pain and
    suffering.*

*Dear all souls who have hurt or harmed
    my ancestors and me in all lifetimes,
I totally and unconditionally forgive you,
    and I humbly ask my ancestors to do
    the same.
I forgive you.
Please forgive me.
Bring love, peace, and harmony.
Thank you. Thank you. Thank you.*

Sound Power. Chant or sing from your heart
with greatest love:

*Da Ai, Da Ai
Da Ai, Da Ai
Da Ai, Da Ai
Da Ai, Da Ai . . .*

Greatest love
Greatest love
Greatest love
Greatest love . . .

Mind Power. Visualize bright golden light shining in your heart and in the hearts of all humanity and all souls.

Tao Source Calligraphy Tracing Power. Apply the Five Fingers Tracing Power Hand Position (figure 2) to trace the *Da Ai* calligraphy following the pathway in figure 3. You can also trace with your body. At the same time, chant *Da Ai*.

Trace for ten minutes per time, at least three times per day. There is no time limit. You can trace as often as you can for as long as you can.

When you do this practice, you are serving Mother Earth, humanity, and countless planets, stars, galaxies, and universes. You are offering your love to humanity and all souls. The more you trace and chant, the better.

Many people wonder how they can help humanity. They want to make a difference yet feel powerless to do so. I share with you, dear reader, that to chant and to trace the *Da Ai* calligraphy within this book and to invite all humanity, Mother Earth, and countless planets, stars, galaxies, and universes to join you to chant is not a small service. It is a very significant service. You will receive blessings from Divine, Tao Source, Heaven, Mother Earth, and countless planets, stars, galaxies, and universes. If millions and billions of people chant *Da Ai,* greatest love, the power of transformation for humanity and Mother Earth cannot be expressed enough.

Sing or chant from your heart while tracing:

Da Ai, Da Ai
Da Ai, Da Ai
Da Ai, Da Ai
Da Ai, Da Ai . . .

Greatest love
Greatest love
Greatest love
Greatest love . . .

I love my heart and soul
I love all humanity
Join hearts and souls together
Love, peace, and harmony
Love, peace, and harmony . . .

Humanity and Mother Earth need Da Ai. All souls need Da Ai. Serve humanity, Mother Earth, and all souls. Join our global chanting for love, peace, and harmony. You can download a beautiful mp3 recording of this powerful song, *Love, Peace and Harmony,* at www.lovepeaceharmony.org.

Let us join hearts and souls together to create a Love Peace Harmony Universal Family.

Thank you. Thank you. Thank you.
Love you. Love you. Love you.

Conclusion

It is my greatest joy and honor to bring these teachings to humanity through this small book. Apply the wisdom. Apply Da Ai, greatest love, to every aspect of your life.

To summarize:

"Shen" includes soul, heart, and mind. Shen is the boss for a human being. Divine and Tao Source are the top leaders for countless souls, including humanity, Mother Earth, Heaven, and countless planets, stars, galaxies, and universes.

This book shares with humanity that Da Ai, greatest love, offers the highest purification and upliftment of shen, which includes soul, heart, and mind; qi, which is energy; and jing, which is matter. Apply Da Ai and the Five Power Techniques, including Body Power, Soul Power, Sound Power, Mind

Power, and Tao Source Calligraphy Tracing
Power.

First give greatest love
Unconditional love
Melts all disasters and challenges
Clears your heart and enlightens
your soul, heart, and mind

Da Tao Zhi Jian, *the Big Way is extremely*
simple.

This pocket-sized book is a practical tool
that you can apply anywhere, anytime, to
enrich and bless your health, relationships,
finances, intelligence, and every aspect of
life. Carry it with you to receive the greatest
benefits.

Apply the Five Power Techniques.

Trace the Tao Source Calligraphy *Da Ai*.

Chant *Da Ai*.

Transform yourself.

Transform your loved ones.

Transform humanity.
Transform Mother Earth.
Transform Heaven.
Transform countless planets, stars, galaxies,
and universes.

Da Ai, Da Ai
Da Ai, Da Ai
Da Ai, Da Ai
Da Ai, Da Ai

Greatest love
Greatest love
Greatest love
Greatest love

I love my heart and soul
I love all humanity
Join hearts and souls together
Love, peace, and harmony
Love, peace, and harmony

About the Authors

Dr. and Master Zhi Gang Sha is a world-renowned healer, Tao Grandmaster, philanthropist, humanitarian, and creator of Tao Calligraphy. He is the founder of Soul Mind Body Medicine™ and an eleven-time *New York Times* bestselling author. An M.D. in China and a doctor of traditional Chinese medicine in China and Canada, Master Sha is the founder of the Tao Academy™ and the Love Peace Harmony Foundation™, which is dedicated to helping families worldwide create happier and healthier lives. A grandmaster of many ancient disciplines, including tai chi, qigong, kung fu, feng shui, and the *I Ching,* Master Sha was named Qigong Master of the Year at the Fifth World Congress on Qigong. In 2006, he was honored with the prestigious Martin Luther King, Jr. Commemorative Commission Award for his humanitarian efforts, and in 2016, Master Sha received rare and prestigious appointments as Shu Fa Jia (National Chinese Calligrapher Master) and Yan Jiu Yuan (Honorable Researcher Professor), the highest titles a Chinese calligrapher can receive, by the State Ethnic of Academy of Painting in China.

A Master Teacher personally trained by Master Sha, **Master Maya Mackie** is dedicated to empowering humanity. She deeply believes that anyone can transform any challenge into an opportunity for growth and, through her great compassion, has helped thousands of people around the world overcome life challenges.

Searching for a comprehensive healing technique that could heal the root cause of sickness or imbalance, Master Maya has studied several healing modalities and aspects of traditional Chinese medicine since an early age. She discovered Master Sha's book *The Power of Soul* in 2009, which led her to study seriously and to devote her life to empowering people to heal themselves and others.

Now one of the top trainers at the Tao Academy, Master Maya teaches people how to apply soul power to every aspect of life, including health, relationships, finances, business, pets, and more.

 **Master Francisco Quintero** is one of the top teachers at the Tao Academy™. As the lead teacher and trainer at the Tao Academy, he has managed and developed worldwide training programs based on the

teachings of Master Sha. Master Francisco's expertise and knowledge have assisted in the training of more than six thousand Tao Hands Practitioners, Soul Teachers and Healers, and Soul Communicators worldwide. He has been featured on German television and BBC Radio, as well as in numerous European publications. As the author of *Divine Joy: How to Experience Joy in Daily Life*, Master Francisco teaches others how to overcome life challenges and create a joyful life using simple yet powerful Tao secrets and practices.

Other Books by Dr. and Master Sha

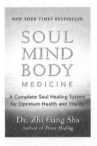

Soul Mind Body Medicine: A Complete Soul Healing System for Optimum Health and Vitality. New World Library, 2006.

What is the real secret to healing and transformation? World-renowned healer Dr. and Master Zhi Gang Sha gives us a simple yet powerful answer to this age-old question:

> Heal the soul first; then healing of the mind and body will follow.®

In *Soul Mind Body Medicine*, Dr. and Master Sha shows that love and forgiveness are the golden keys to soul healing. From that foundation, he presents practical tools to heal and transform soul, mind, and body. The techniques and the underlying theories are easy to learn and practice and profoundly effective. They include:

- Self-healing methods for more than one hundred conditions, from the common cold to back pain to heart disease to diabetes
- Step-by-step approaches to weight loss, recovery from chronic illness, emotional balance, and maintenance of good health
- A revolutionary one-minute healing technique

The Power of Soul: The Way to Heal, Rejuvenate, Transform, and Enlighten All Life. Heaven's Library/Atria, 2009. Also available as an audiobook and a trade paperback.

The third book of the Soul Power Series is the flagship of the entire series.

The Power of Soul empowers you to understand, develop, and apply the power of soul for healing, prevention of sickness, rejuvenation, transformation of every aspect of life (including relationships and finances), and soul enlightenment. It also empowers you to develop soul wisdom and soul intelligence, and to apply Soul Orders for healing and transformation of every aspect of life.

This book teaches Divine Soul Downloads (specifically, Divine Soul Transplants) for the first time in history. A Divine Soul Transplant is the divine way to heal, rejuvenate, and transform every aspect of a human being's life and the life of all universes.

This book offers eleven permanent Divine Soul Transplants as a gift to every reader. Includes bonus Soul Song for Rejuvenation mp3 download.

Soul Healing Miracles: Ancient and New Sacred Wisdom, Knowledge, and Practical Techniques for Healing the Spiritual, Mental, Emotional, and Physical Bodies. Heaven's Library/BenBella Books, 2013. Also available as an audiobook.

Millions of people on Mother Earth are suffering from sicknesses in their spiritual, mental, emotional, and physical bodies.

Millions of people have limited or no access to health care. They want solutions.

Soul Healing Miracles teaches and empowers humanity to create soul healing miracles. Readers learn sacred wisdom and apply practical techniques. This book includes nine calligraphies written by Master Sha. Everyone can create his or her own soul healing miracles.